AF481157

THE TOP 10 MOST FAMOUS CHEMISTS OF ALL TIME

6TH GRADE CHEMISTRY

Children's Chemistry Books

Speedy Publishing LLC

40 E. Main St. #1156

Newark, DE 19711

www.speedypublishing.com

In this book, we're going to cover details about the lives of ten of the most famous chemists of all time. So, let's get right to it.

Chemists performing an experiment

WHAT DO CHEMISTS DO?

Chemists explore the nature of substances and how they change under varying conditions. The knowledge that chemists gain through research is used in all different types of industries.

FAMOUS CHEMISTS

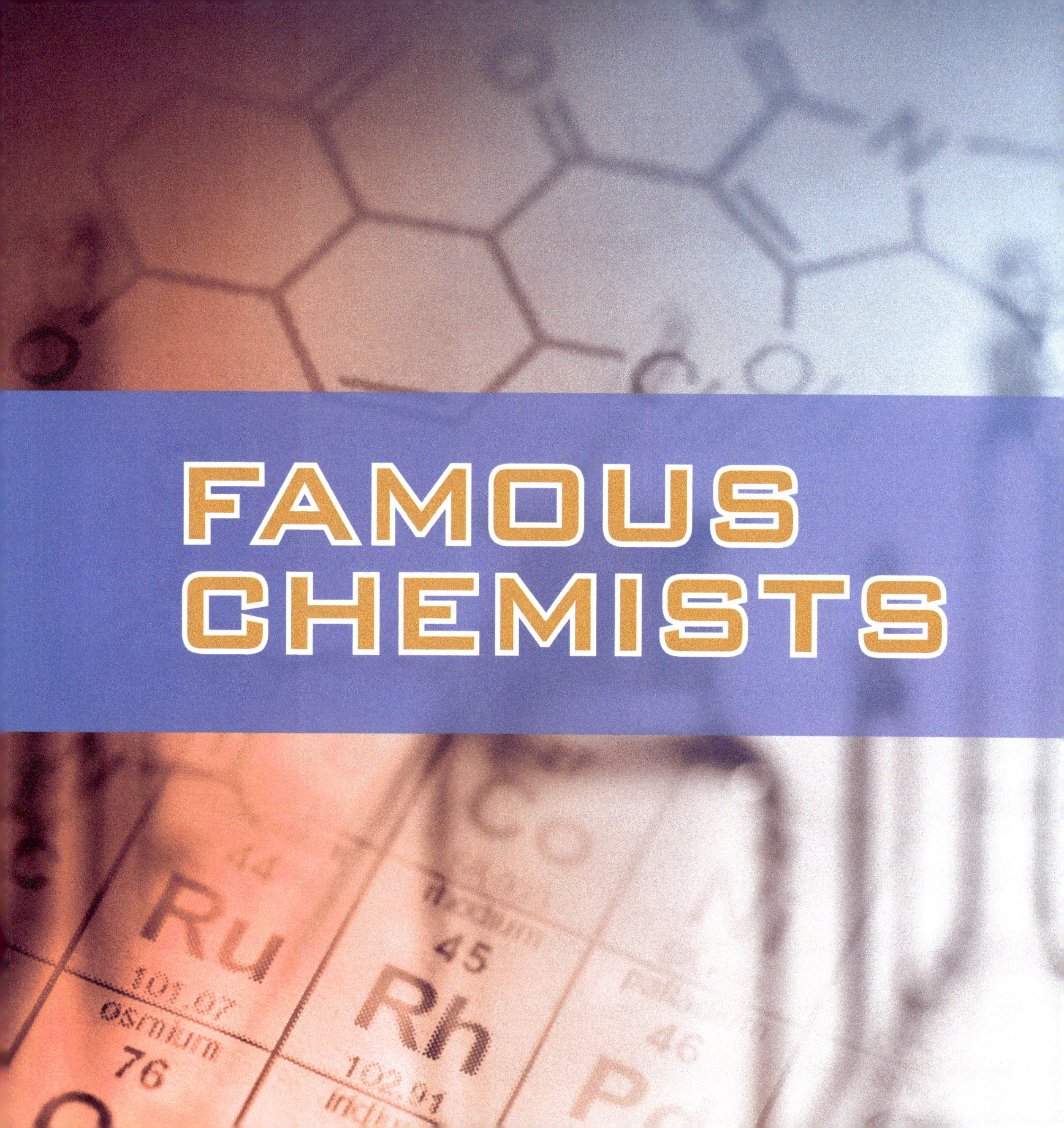

Amadeo Avogadro

AMEDEO AVOGADRO

Born in 1776, the Italian chemist Amedeo Avogadro was part of a family of distinguished lawyers. He practiced law until he realized that he had a passion for the natural sciences. Avogadro did a lot of experimentation with different types of gases.

He discovered through his experiments that if equal volumes of gases are subjected to the same exact conditions of pressure and temperature, they will contain the same number of molecules. This important law was eventually named after him.

Avogadro's Law

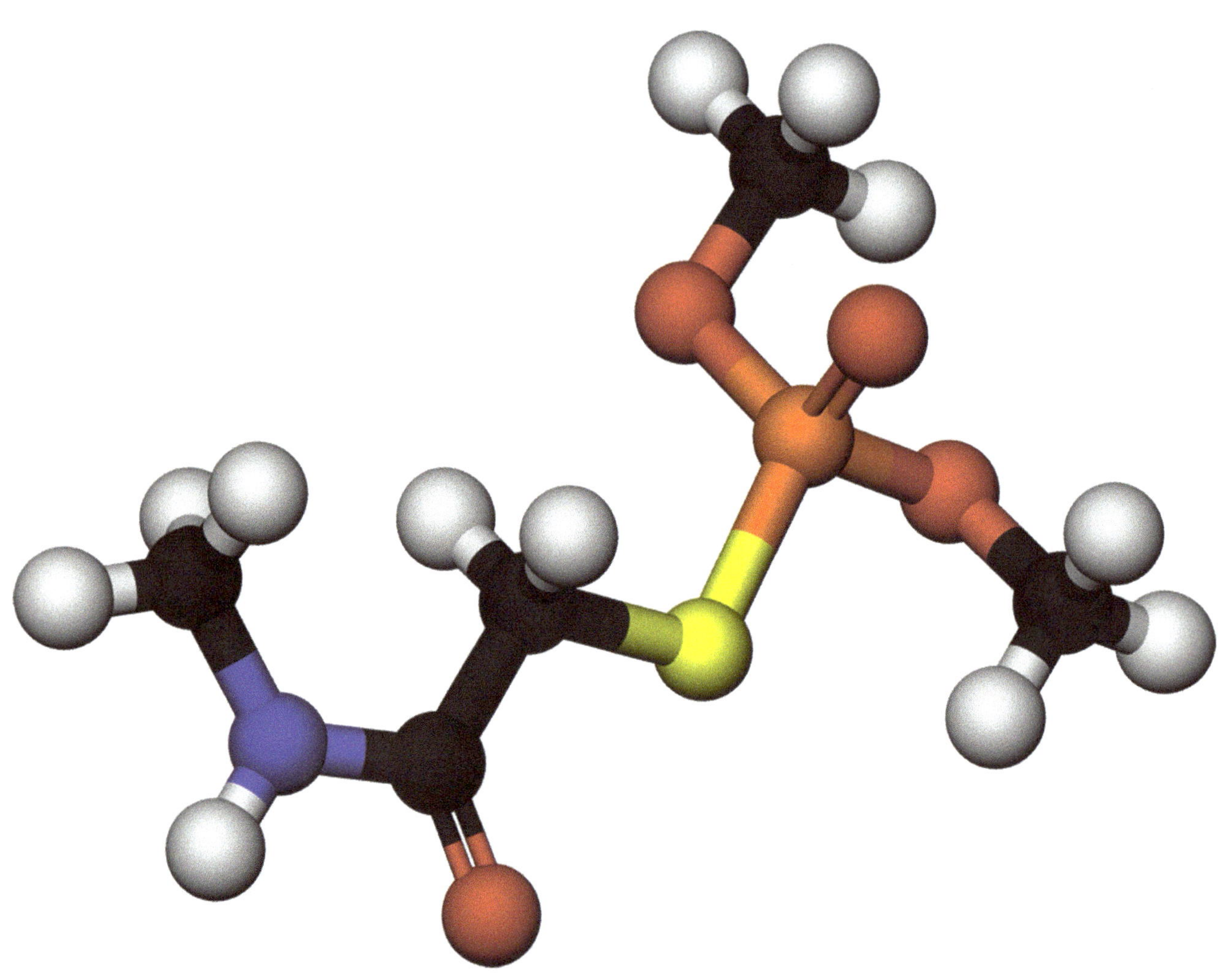

Hydrogen Isotopes

He was the very first scientist to understand that elements existed in the form of molecules and that these molecules were made of individual atoms.

In 1811, he wrote the correct molecular formulas for water as well as ammonia, hydrogen chloride, and carbon monoxide. He's recognized at the founder of modern atomic-molecular theory. The unit of measure called a mole, which is one gram of molecular weight, was named Avogadro's number.

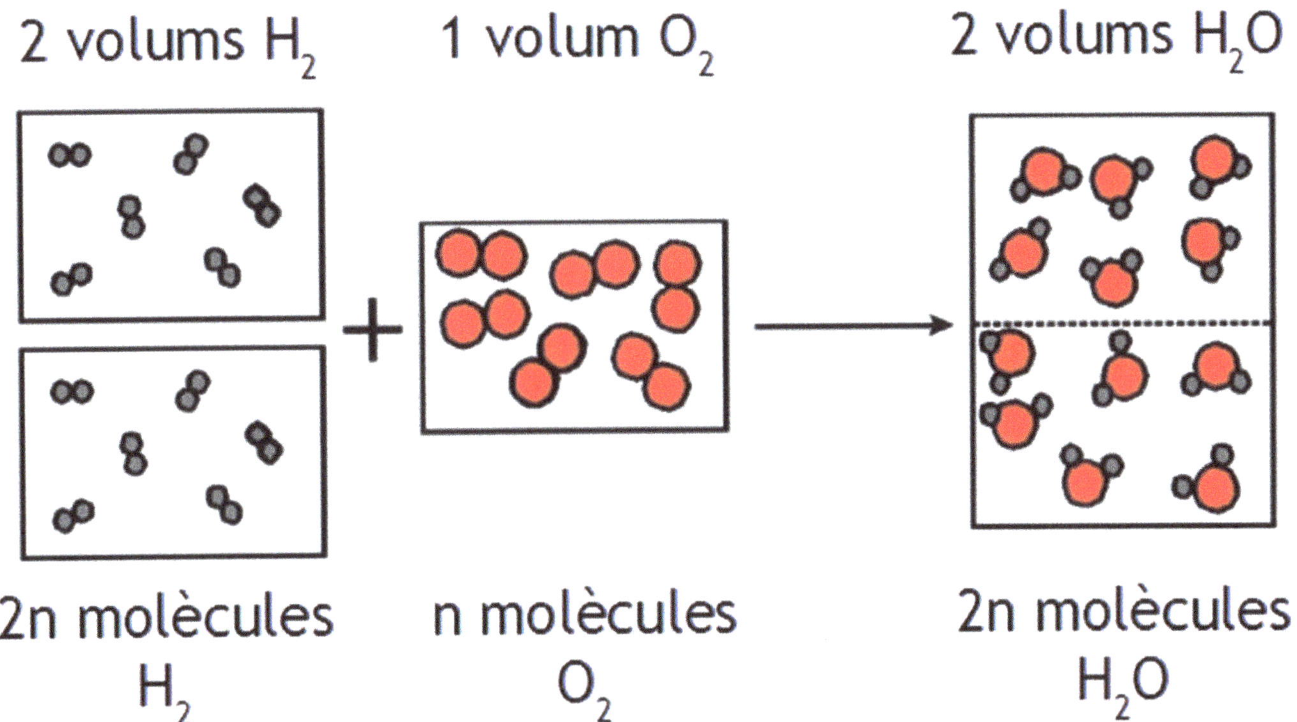

Molecular Formula of Water

Jons Jacob Berzelius

JONS JACOB BERZELIUS

Born in 1779, the Swedish chemist Jons Jacob Berzelius is known as the inventor of the chemical notation we use today. By using the letters from Latin and Greek for the names of the elements and then using number subscripts, he created a useful and compact way to show chemical equations. The number subscripts stood for the number of atoms of each element that were present in a compound.

Along with two other famous chemists in this list, Dalton and Lavoisier, he's thought of as one of the fathers of modern chemistry. He did his training as a medical doctor and took a position as a professor at Stockholm University in 1807.

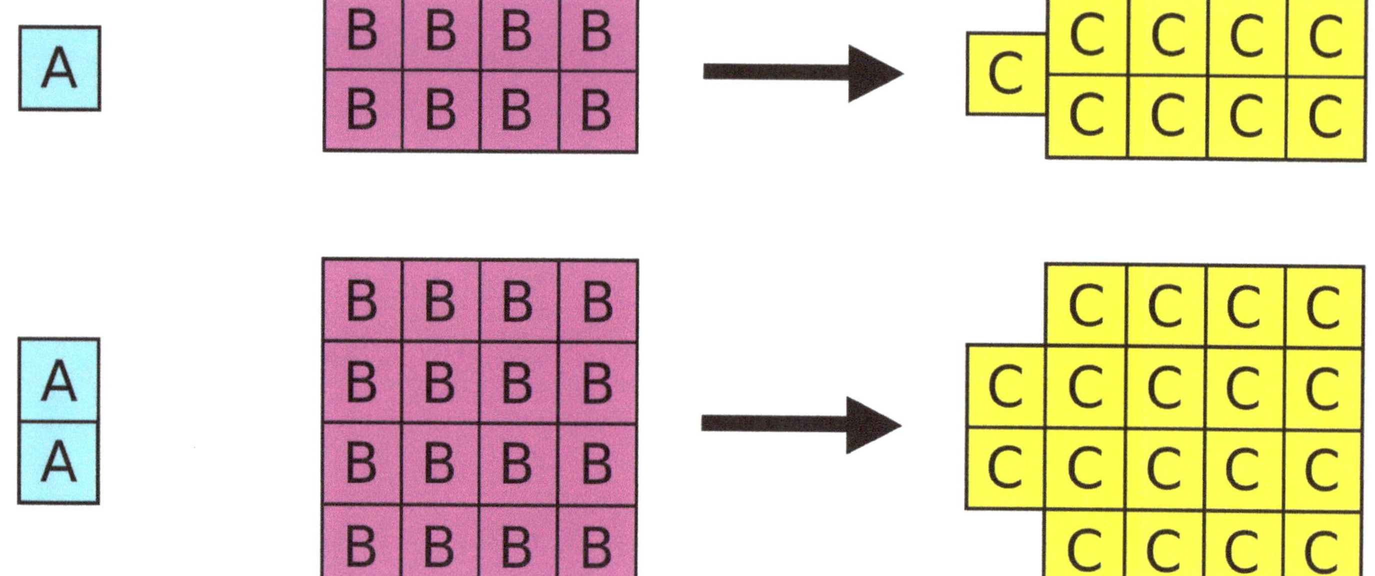

The Law of Constant Proportions

Soon after he arrived he wrote an extensive chemistry textbook for his students. As he was writing his textbook, he discovered what was to become known as the law of constant proportions. This law states that inorganic substances are made up of varying elements that are in constant proportions by weight.

ROBERT BOYLE

Born in 1627, the English chemist Robert Boyle helped to champion the scientific method as we know it today. During the English Civil Wars, he studied at Oxford and was constantly reading and experimenting along with his research associates.

Robert Boyle

*Albert Einstein (center)
with other scientists*

This group of scientists was dedicated to the "New Philosophy." This way of thinking supported the idea that careful observations and experiments were the key to scientific understanding and were more important than mere logical thinking. Once the British reign was restored in 1660, he helped to found the Royal Society to pursue this new scientific method.

In 1660 Boyle wrote a book on the physical nature of air. He devised a beautifully constructed series of experiments that used an air pump to create a vacuum. When he revised the second edition of this work two years later, he included what was later called Boyle's Law. The law stated that the volume of a gas is inversely proportional to its pressure.

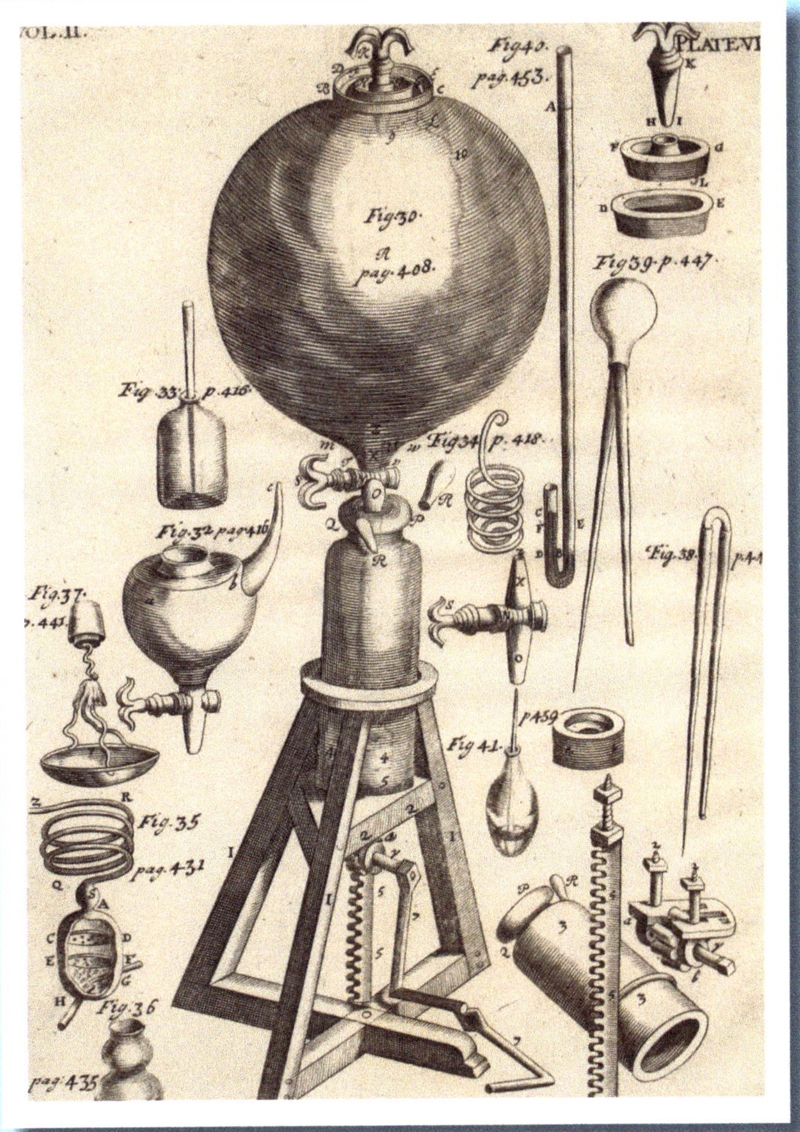

Boyle's Series of Experiments

Marie Curie

Born in 1867, the Polish chemist Marie Curie was a pioneer researcher in the study of radioactivity, a word she herself coined. Along with her husband, Pierre, who was also a famous chemist, she discovered the radioactive elements polonium and radium. In 1903, they received the Nobel Prize in physics. That same year she was the first woman in Europe to earn a Ph.D. in physics. She received the Nobel Prize again, this time for chemistry, in the year 1911.

Marie was fascinated by reports about the discovery of X-rays. She had read findings that stated that uranium ores gave off rays as well. Marie had a hypothesis that these rays were an atomic property of the element of uranium. If her theory were true, it would mean that the atom wasn't the smallest fragment of matter. As we know today, she was correct, the atom is made up of smaller components.

Marie Curie

Marie Curie in Her Laboratory

When the first World War broke out in 1914, she stopped her research for a while to help coordinate X-ray machines to help physicians at the front. Sadly, at that time nothing was known about the dangers of being exposed to radiation. She died of a blood disease due to her years of radiation exposure.

JOHN DALTON

Born in 1766, the English chemist John Dalton was influential in developing the fundamental atomic theory concerning elements and their atomic composition. He was a schoolteacher and an expert on color blindness. His interest in chemistry was actually sparked by his interest in weather records.

John Dalton

He kept daily records of the weather from the year 1787 until his death. As he learned more about the composition of air, he proposed that when gases that don't react with each other are mixed together, the total pressure they exert is the same as the sum of the partial pressures of the individual gases. This law is now named for him. Dalton also found the atomic weights for many substances.

SIR HUMPHRY DAVY

Born in 1778, the English chemist Humphry Davy is best known for his discoveries of both chlorine and iodine. He was also responsible for inventing the Davy lamp, which allowed miners a safe way to work closely with gases that are flammable.

He used electrolysis, a technique using a direct electric current to create chemical reactions that don't happen naturally, to isolate and thus discover many critical elements, such as calcium and magnesium.

Sir Humphry Davy

His publication, "Researches, Chemical and Philosophical, chiefly concerning Nitrous Oxide and its Respiration," documented his research on laughing gas and he did extensive research on other gases, such as hydrogen and nitrogen as well. He was considered to be one of the greatest inventors and chemists from Great Britain.

ROSALIND FRANKLIN

Born in 1920, the English chemist Rosalind Franklin is known today for her pioneering work in X-ray diffraction, which is the scattering of X-rays by the atoms of a crystal. This technique is useful in obtaining information about a crystal's structure.

Rosalind Franklin

DNA Strand

Franklin applied these techniques to DNA fibers and got an image of the double helix structure of the DNA strand. The photo she took, called **photo 51**, was taken from her files without her knowledge and became an essential clue in the understanding of and further discoveries about DNA by Watson and Crick. She also researched polio and other viruses, such as the tobacco mosaic virus.

ANTOINE LAVOISIER

Born in 1743, the French chemist Antoine Lavoisier was born into a wealthy family of aristocrats. He set up a lab in Paris in 1775 to test different experiments that he created. He was one of the first chemists, along with Berzelius and Dalton, who believed that data and precision in experiments was critical. Along with the other two chemists, he's considered one of the founders of modern chemistry.

Antoine Lavoisier

Sir Antoine Lavoisier and His Wife

At the time, scientists thought that fire was made up of an element called **phlogiston**. It was Lavoisier who discovered that oxygen was critical to combustion. He also proved that mass isn't destroyed by chemical reactions. This law is called the law of conservation of mass. Much of his work led to the continued work on the periodic table.

DMITRI MENDELEYEV

Born in 1834, the Russian chemist Dmitri Mendeleyev is known today for creating the organization of the periodic table in its more modern form. He discovered the principles for organizing the table while he was writing a textbook called The Principles of Chemistry for his students at the University of St. Petersburg.

Dmitri Mendeleyev

He noticed certain patterns that were happening within specific groups of elements. Using his advanced knowledge of the properties of these elements, he was able to connect them further. He organized them into a grid by their atomic weights.

At the time he proposed the periodic table, other scientists were not very supportive. But based on his periodic law, Mendeleyev was able to make predictions about other elements that had not yet been found! When these predictions came true in the discoveries found decades later, his periodic table was accepted and is still used today.

PERIODIC TABLE OF THE ELEMENTS

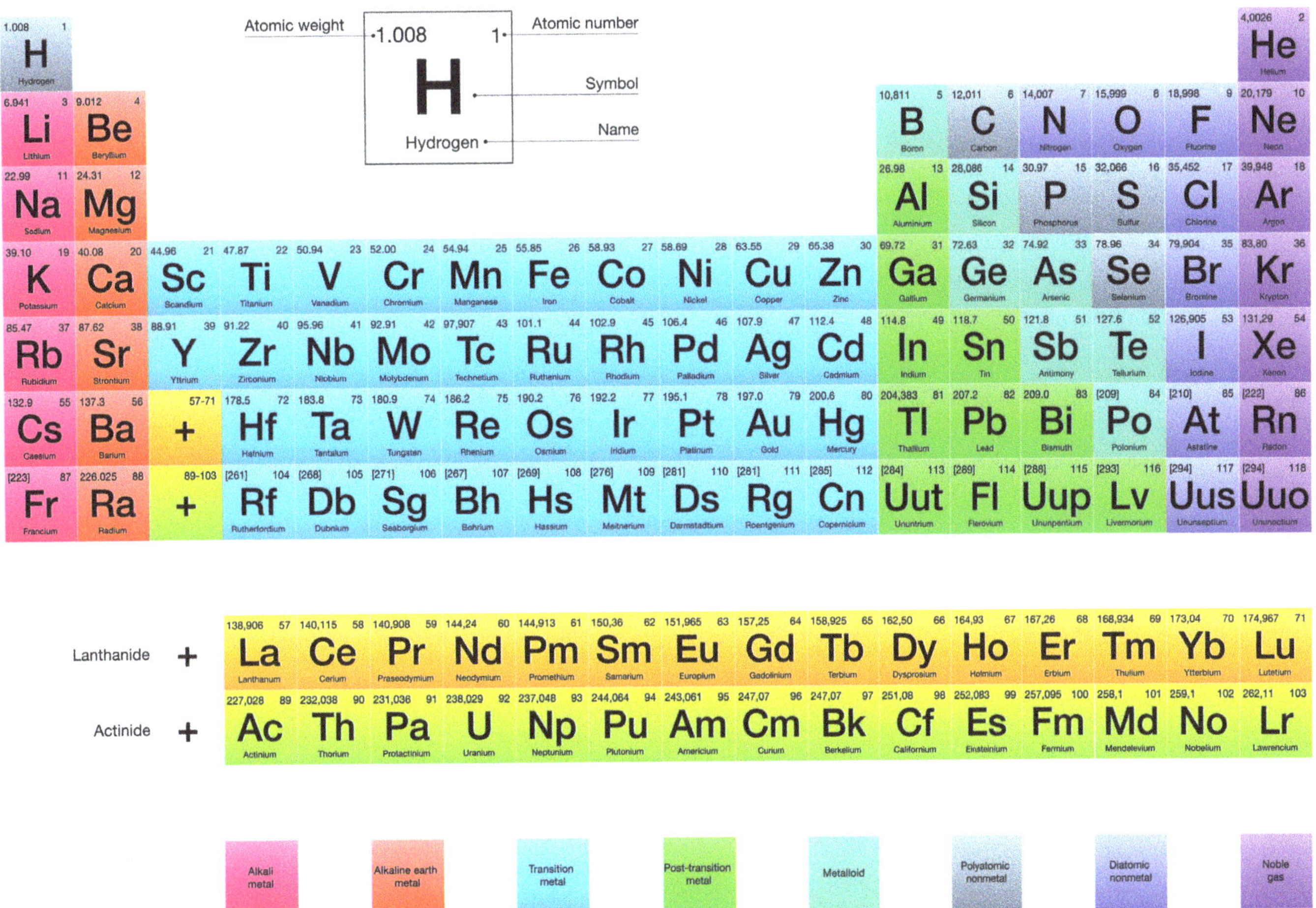

Alfred Nobel

ALFRED NOBEL

Born in 1833, the Swedish chemist Alfred Nobel held over 300 patents for his inventions throughout his lifetime. As a young man, Alfred worked at his father's factory, which created arms and ammunition. In 1864, Alfred's younger brother was killed at the factory. Alfred vowed to find a safer way for explosives to work. Through his work he was able to develop dynamite, which was much safer than previous explosives to use.

When a second of Alfred's brothers died, the newspapers in France published Alfred's obituary by mistake. The paper condemned him for inventing dynamite. Alfred was horrified that this would be how he would be remembered when he died so he left the equivalent of 250 million dollars for science prizes to be given in his name—the Nobel Prizes that we know today.

Nobel Piece Prize Award Medal

Awesome! Now you know more about some of the most important chemists throughout history. You can find more Chemistry Books from Baby Professor by searching the website of your favorite book retailer.

Visit
BABY PROFESSOR
EDUCATION KIDS
www.BabyProfessorBooks.com
to download Free Baby Professor eBooks and view
our catalog of new and exciting Children's Books